SECRETS OF
NATURE

by
Jennifer Cochrane

Designed by David Nash

Illustrators
Graham Allen · Mike Atkinson
Pat Lenander · Bernard Robinson · David Wright

Ray Rourke Publishing Company, Inc.
Windermere, Florida 32786

5248

Published by Ray Rourke Publishing Company, Inc.
Windermere, Florida 32786
Copyright © 1979 Piper Books Ltd.
Copyright © 1981 Ray Rourke Publishing Company, Inc.

Library of Congress Cataloging in Publication Data

Cochrane, Jennifer.
  Secrets of nature.

  SUMMARY: Brief text and illustrations explore the
characteristics, habits, and various other aspects of
plant and animal life.
  1. Animals—Juvenile literature.   2. Plants—Juvenile
literature.   [1. Animals.   2. Plants]   I. Allen, Graham,
1940-   .   II. Title.
QL49.C65   1981   591   81-107
ISBN 0-86592-072-9   AACR1

Contents

woodpecker

Crossbills gnaw small crab apples to eat the seeds at the core.

squirrel

A herring gull track. The middle toe in the webbed foot is about 2½ inches.

field vole

roe deer

gnawed roots

otter

A nut left by a wood mouse shows that it is turned during gnawing.

Adult squirrels make a small hole at the top of a nut before cracking it open.

Tracks and Signs

There are plenty of wild animals even in cities. But we seldom see them. Many birds and small animals live in our parks and gardens. Of course, there are far more in the fields and woods. They leave evidence of their passing and we often miss it. We need to know what to look for and where to look.

A tree may be a home to birds, insects and small mammals. Sometimes you will see a bird's nest or a squirrel's drey in the branches. In a hole high up in the trunk there may be owls or bats. A family of field voles or dormice may make their grassy nests around the roots. On the ground, foxes and badgers may have left tell-tale foot-prints or droppings.

If you are lucky, you may find owl pellets. These are little balls made up of the bones and fur from the owl's prey. Perhaps you may even find the sloughed skin of a snake. Snakes shed their outer skins when they grow. If you know where to look and are prepared to be patient, the secrets of nature are there to be found.

In its search for insects and grubs the woodpecker hacks the bark off trees leaving clear bill marks. The squirrel strips the bark to reach the soft layer underneath but does not eat the bark. In winter the field vole will eat the bark it gnaws off the foot of treetrunks. The roots of young trees are another source of food for the field vole.

The roe deer marks its territory by fraying bark with its antlers. A slide on a snowy or muddy bank may be a sign that otters have been playing.

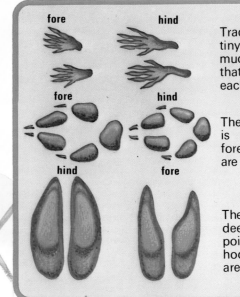

fore   hind

fore   hind

hind   fore

Tracks made by the tiny shrew in soft mud or snow show that it has five toes on each foot.

The hind-foot of a fox is smaller than the fore-foot. The claws are long and pointed.

The track of the roe deer shows the pointed shape of the hoofs. The front hoofs are splayed.

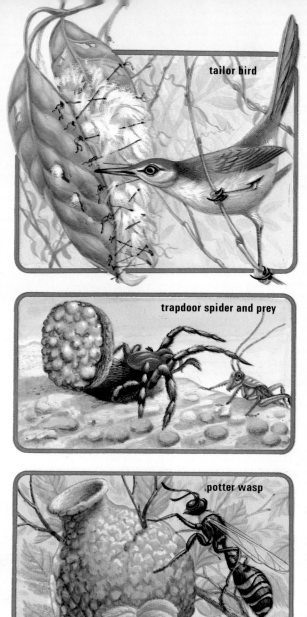

tailor bird

trapdoor spider and prey

potter wasp

Animal Homes

Most animals do not need a real home. They only use nests or dens to shelter their young. The rest of the year they wander in search of food. A few "social" animals live in large groups. They build colonies and may use them for many years. Lemmings, prairie dogs and rabbits live together in such colonies underground.

An animal may not only build a home to protect its young. Some animals build homes to trap their prey. The burrow of the trapdoor spider is a good example. Other animals build homes to store their food. The honey pots of the potter wasp are "larder" homes.

Not all birds make nests. The guillemot lays its eggs on a bare rock. The curlew nests on the ground. But the tailor bird is a skillful nest-builder. It sews leaves together with a long stem of a plant to make a swinging cradle for its eggs.

Finding the right place to build a home is very important. A home must be safe and it must be near food. When there are many suitable "building sites" in an area lots of animals can make their homes there.

a lemming colony

The beavers of North America make such fine homes that they are known as the master builders of the animal world. They build their island homes on lakes and rivers. We call them lodges. Beavers are expert dam-builders too. They dam rivers to make a pool before they begin work on the lodge. Families of beavers toil together to complete their home before winter comes.

Gnawing with their sharp, chisel-like teeth, the beavers fell trees. Then they cut the trunks and branches into logs and float them into position. A single dam may need hundreds of tons of wood. The beavers cement the logs together with clay and leaves to make the dam strong.

They build the lodge with the same care. A beaver lodge looks like a mound of sticks and mud. Above the level of the water it may have two or more chambers. All the entrances to the lodge are under water so the beavers can come and go in safety when the lake freezes. In the fall they store juicy shoots and bark near the lodge to eat during the long winter. Inside their sturdy home they need not fear the hungry lynx prowling overhead.

Animal Life Stories

The most important time in an animal's life is its mating and breeding season. Each year enough young must be produced to replace those which have died. In this way the population stays about the same. If a group of animals cannot produce enough young to make up the number, it quickly dwindles. It may be in danger of dying out altogether.

nucleus

Above: The amoeba is a tiny water-living animal with only one cell. After the nucleus splits, the whole cell divides to make two amoebae.

Below: A butterfly egg hatches into an eating stage called a larva or caterpillar. After eating leaves all summer the caterpillar weaves a silk case around itself and becomes a chrysalis. The following spring, a fully grown butterfly emerges ready to begin the cycle again.

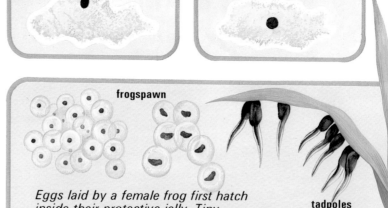

frogspawn

tadpoles

Eggs laid by a female frog first hatch inside their protective jelly. Tiny tadpoles then leave the jelly to hang on the leaves of water plants by their suckers. As they grow they develop back legs then front legs before they lose their tails and become frogs.

caterpillar

red admiral butterfly

egg

chrysalis

The sea turtle leaves her eggs to hatch in a sandy "nest". When they hatch the babies have to fend for themselves. In danger from hungry birds they race towards the sea.

froglet

Kangaroos are marsupials. They carry their babies in pouches. When a baby is born it crawls blind and helpless into its mother's pouch, feeds on her milk and stays there until it is quite large.

Some lowly animals do not need to mate. Amoeba is a tiny animal that simply splits in two to make a new amoeba. But most animals need both males and females to reproduce. The female produces the eggs. Then she mates with a male who fertilizes her eggs with sperm.

Many creatures lay so many eggs that some are sure to survive to become adults. Butterflies, frogs and sea turtles all lay large numbers of eggs. Baby turtles look like their parents when they hatch. But some creatures go through different stages and forms before they finally become fully developed.

Animals and their Young

Different animals have different ways of ensuring that their kind will survive. Some lay so many eggs that there is a good chance of a few young surviving. So there is no need for the parents to care for them. Very few fishes look after their eggs and young. Most fishes lay their eggs and leave their hundreds of babies to fend for themselves.

However, there are many excellent parents in the animal world. Birds and mammals do not normally have large families. But they take good care of their young. In this way, young animals have a good chance of survival.

Birds sit on their eggs to hatch them. They bring food to the chicks until they are able to fly. The chicks have to stay in the nest until they molt their fluffy down. Then their feathers grow. When they have wing feathers they are able to fly and find their own food.

Only a few mammals, such as cattle, horses and antelope, have babies that can run about soon after they are born. Most mammal babies are born helpless, often blind and naked. Their parents must feed and protect them for weeks or months.

koala bear and baby

When a herring gull chick needs food it pecks at the red spot on the bill of the adult. This stimulates the adult to give food to the hungry chick.

Mouthbreeder

merganser and young

Most mammals and birds take good care of their young. The koala bear and the merganser carry babies on their backs. Few fishes care for their young. But the mouthbreeder does by sheltering them in his mouth when danger threatens. He spits them out when it is safe.

A herd of musk oxen works together to protect the young. If they are under attack from a pack of hungry wolves they stand in a circle facing out. The young are safe inside the circle.

Energy from the Sun

Animals either eat plants or they eat other animals that feed on plants. But plants can make their own food.

Plants need the sun to make food. They use the energy of sunlight in their food-making process. Taking water from the soil and carbon dioxide, a gas, from the air, they use sunlight to change them into sugar which they need to grow. This process is called photosynthesis. It takes place mainly in the leaves which contain chlorophyll, a green pigment. It is chlorophyll which absorbs light energy from the sun. During the process of photosynthesis plants produce a gas called oxygen. Animals need oxygen to breathe. So photosynthesis helps animals to live.

Roots anchor a plant to the ground. They also absorb water and mineral salts and, sometimes, store food. There are two main kinds of roots. Fibrous roots are busy systems that often spread deep underground. The foxglove has fibrous roots. Tap roots like the long, thick root of the carrot are used to store food.

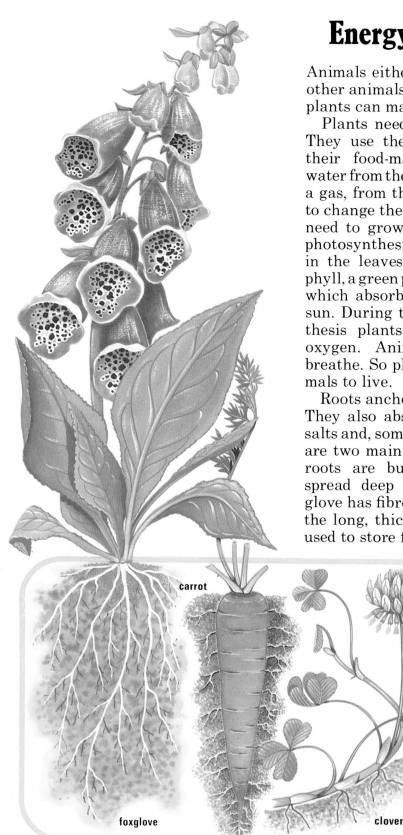

carrot

crocus

foxglove

clover

sundew

Above: The sundew gets some of its food by trapping insects and digesting their bodies. Right: Unlike green plants, mushrooms do not need the sun. They cannot make their own food but feed on wood and dead plant matter.

Above: Most plants grow towards the light and many flowers turn to follow the path of the sun. Below: A cross-section of a leaf shows the layers of cells inside. A plant makes food in its leaves and breathes through them.

Old Plant to New

Most flowers make seeds from which new plants grow. A flower needs pollen from another flower of the same kind before it can make seeds, unless it can pollinate itself. Pollen is sometimes carried from one flower to another by insects. Attracted by brightly colored flowers, they settle on them to search for nectar. As they do this, their bodies pick up powdery pollen. When the insect visits the next flower, some of the pollen brushes off and fertilizes the plant so that new seeds can be made. Some plants are pollinated by wind.

Plants cannot move about so they need help to spread their seeds around. The wind plays an important part in scattering seeds such as the sycamore and the light, downy "parachutes" of the thistle and the dandelion.

Animals help seeds to travel, too. Some seeds are hidden inside tasty fruit, and pass through an animal's body after being eaten. Others have tiny hooks or burrs. They catch on to a furry animal and travel with it to other places. In these ways new plants can often grow far from their parent plants.

New plant life begins in various ways. Brightly colored flowers (**1**) are pollinated by insects, whereas dull colorless flowers, such as grass, are wind-pollinated. Poppy seeds are carried in a head like a pepper-pot (**2**). When shaken by the wind the seeds scatter. Fungi spores are also wind-borne, as are the seeds of reedmaces (**3**), the "parachute" seeds of dandelions (**4**) and thistles (**5**), and winged sycamore seeds (**6**). Animals help disperse some seeds. Squirrels bury acorns then often forget them (**7**); a pecking goldfinch may shake plantain seeds off their stalks (**8**); and the mistle thrush (**9**), while eating mistletoe berries, may get the gummy seeds stuck to its beak. If the bird wipes these off on another tree a new plant may grow.

Above: How a bean grows. First the root begins to grow downwards. Then the leaf-bearing shoot grows up towards the sunlight.

Balance of Nature

Nothing is wasted in nature. The food that plants make from sunlight passes to animals and then into the soil. The soil then feeds the plants so that the cycle can begin again. When an animal eats a plant it eats all the food made by the plant. If the animal is then eaten by another animal, the same food is passed on again. When an animal dies, its body rots. It is broken up by tiny bacteria. This food passes into the soil and nourishes growing plants.

"Food chains" can be long and complicated. A simple food chain is shown in the picture opposite. Aphids feed on the juices from a rose bush. A ladybug feeds on the aphids and is then caught and eaten by a spider. A hungry shrew makes a meal of the spider. Shrews are hunted and eaten by owls. Each of the animals in the food chain depends on the food made in the rose bush.

Some animals live on what others pass out in their droppings. Among these is the scarab, or dung beetle. It makes a ball of dung larger than itself and rolls it away to eat in its burrow.

The balance of nature can be upset. Sometimes the number of animals outstrips the food supply. The lemming population often explodes and the lemmings migrate in search of food. Many of them starve or are drowned. But those that are left can live better because they are not overcrowded.

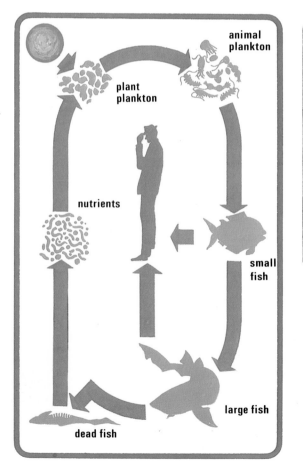

The balance of nature was upset in Australia when rabbits were introduced. They bred rapidly and turned rich pasture into desert, depriving themselves and other animals of food.

Left: Plant plankton in the sea uses sunlight to make its food. It is eaten by animal plankton which feeds fishes, some of which are eaten by larger fishes, others by man. When fish die, their bodies are broken down by bacteria and nutrients rise to the surface to help feed plankton.

lemmings

dung beetle

How Animals Move

All animals move—on land, in water or through the air. Those that live in water either float or swim. The water helps to support their bodies. Most swimmers use their limbs (fins or flippers) or tails as paddles. Even tiny one-celled animals use their whip-like tails for swimming or row themselves along by fanning tiny hairs on their bodies. The jellyfish opens and shuts itself like an umbrella to propel itself. Most fishes' bodies are shaped so that they can move through water easily.

A moth caterpillar takes "steps" with its whole body.

Land animals need bony skeletons to hold their bodies firm. Most mammals are four-legged. Only man and the apes have mastered walking erect on two legs leaving the hands free.

Insects have six legs, spiders eight, and millipedes many more. These animals move their legs in pairs and can run very swiftly. Snakes and worms have no legs at all. Worms move by using bristles and plates on their skin to pull themselves along the ground.

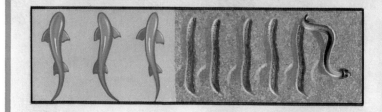

Most fishes flick their strong tails from side to side to drive them through the water. Fins are used for steering.

A sidewinder snake moves fast over the sand. Only a small part of its body touches the ground at one time as it slithers along.

18

The hydra is a tiny animal that usually stays in one spot. It moves by turning over on its "arms".

The flying squirrel cannot really fly. It glides, using the skin stretched between its legs like a wing. When a bird flies, its wings beat the air, keeping it aloft and pushing it along. The air below the wings helps to push the bird upwards as it flies.

The scallop can swim about by flapping the two halves of its shell together. It can move fast by clapping shut violently, shooting out jets of water as it propels itself forwards.

Birds and insects are masters of the air. But some snakes, lizards, frogs, squirrels, mice and fish are said to "fly". In fact, these animals only glide. They cannot gain height. True fliers like birds, insects and bats can create "lift" by flapping their wings. To fly well, a bird must be very strong as well as fairly light. The feathers covering its body not only keep it warm but give the smooth, broad wing surface necessary for flight.

19

Woodland Presbyterian School

Beaks and Feet

A bird's beak and feet are good clues to its way of life. The woodpecker's hooked claws cling to the bark of trees while its strong beak drills into the wood for insects. The reed warbler can grasp slender reed stems. Walking on floating lily leaves is easy for the water rail. Its weight is well balanced on its long, widespread toes.

reed warbler

water rail

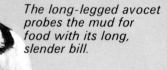

The long-legged avocet probes the mud for food with its long, slender bill.

woodpecker

eagle

Far left: Seed-eating birds like the hawfinch have sturdy beaks to crack open hard nuts and seeds.

Right: The swift catches its food—small insects—on the wing. It follows them through the air with its wide beak always open and ready to catch.

Right: The crossbill's beak acts as a lever to open pine cones. It strips the scales from the cone with its beak, and takes out the seeds with its tongue.

Left: The grouse grows a fringe of feathers around its feet in winter. This acts like a pair of snowshoes.

Left: The duck's webbed feet push it through the water.
Right: The flamingo's bill sifts food from soft mud.

1 Katydid mimicking lichen

2 Purple thorn moth caterpillar mimicking a twig

3 Treble bar moth on tree bark

4 Cossid moth mimicking flower

5 Owlet moth and dead leaves

6 Leaf bug

7 Thorn tree hoppers look like thorns

8 Stick insect

9 Orchid mantis mimicking a tropical flower

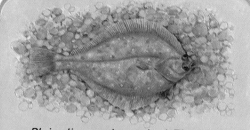

Antelopes and other open country grazers have dark backs and light bellies. This disguises the shadow on their undersides. The whole animal blends with the grass it feeds on.

Plaice live on the seabed. They cannot swim fast, but use their coloring to escape enemies. The color of their flat bodies can change to match the sandy seabed so they are hard to see.

Animals in Hiding

There are two good reasons why an animal finds it useful to hide. It can avoid being eaten and it can catch its own food by lying in wait for unwary victims. Among the most successful players of animal "hide and seek" are those that use camouflage and mimicry. They match their surroundings or look like parts of a plant. So they fool their enemies.

Some animals are roughly the same color as the trees and plants where they live. Grasshoppers and tree snakes are green to match the leaves. Polar bears living in the snowy Arctic are white.

Vivid color schemes can be very effective. The chameleon hides by changing color to match its surroundings. The deadly Gaboon viper has a startling square and diamond pattern that makes it hard to see. The bold stripes on a zebra confuse an enemy; it is difficult to see where one zebra begins and another ends in a herd.

Fishes face danger from above (from birds) and from below (from other fish). So many of them have dark upper sides and light-colored bellies. The dark blends with the sea, making the fish difficult to spot from the air. And the silvery belly blends with the sunlight above so that it is difficult to pick out from underneath. In the sunny tropical seas, fishes are often brightly colored. Their bold patterns help to break up their shapes among the corals and sponges. this is a good defense against predators.

4

5

Some insects have clever ways of protecting themselves against their enemies. Some are camouflaged so that they are hard to see against the bark on which they live. Others are hidden from danger not only by their color but by their shape as well. These are mimics. They look so much like plants that they trick their enemies again and again.

9

The tiger lives in sunny open grasslands. Its stripes blend with the shadows of trees and tall grass. So smaller animals are unaware that the tiger lies in wait for them.

Escape and Defense

The simplest way for some animals to escape from danger is to run faster than their predators. Many creatures—ostriches, horses, antelopes and many others—rely on speed. Most of them have sharp eyes and ears to warn them that predators are near.

Most small animals hide from danger in burrows or in the undergrowth. Young ones are often hidden in safe places by their parents until they can fend for themselves. Timid creatures simply "freeze" when danger is at hand. By keeping perfectly still, deer fawns have a good chance of staying alive. Their coloring acts as camouflage so they are very difficult to detect unless they move.

Some animals are brightly colored to warn hunters that they are poisonous or that they taste nasty. Their bold markings are called "warning colors". Bees and wasps have yellow and black stripes to warn hungry birds that they risk being stung. Poisonous coral snakes are yellow, black and red.

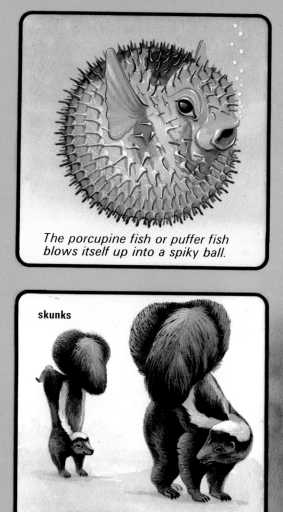

The porcupine fish or puffer fish blows itself up into a spiky ball.

skunks

The frilled lizard of Australia frightens away its enemies by opening out the large collar round its neck. This is a good form of defense because it makes the lizard look large and fearsome. Above right: The skunk defends itself by squirting an evil-smelling fluid at its attackers.

One family of mollusks has a dramatic form of defense. Squids and octopuses squirt out a cloud of ink. While an attacker is confused by this "smoke screen", the squid escapes by jet propulsion.

Many lizards can break off their tails when attacked. The wriggling tail holds the attacker's attention while the lizard escapes. It will grow a new tail eventually.

The pangolin's scaly armor protects it when it rolls into a tight ball.

Warning colors provide such a good defense that animals which are neither poisonous nor unpleasant to eat have copied animals with these colors. There are harmless flies which look exactly like wasps, and non-poisonous milk snakes that look just like coral snakes. This kind of animal trickery is called mimicry.

Other clever tricks are sometimes used to frighten or repel an enemy. The puffer fish pretends to be bigger; the opossum 'plays dead'. Armadillos and pangolins curl up into spiny balls, while hedgehogs have sharp spines.

Animal Partners

eagle and starling

Every animal relies on other creatures in some way. Some find safety in numbers. The huge herds of zebras, gazelles, wildebeestes, giraffes and other animals that roam the plains of Africa find it safer to live together. Other animals sometimes find that it is convenient to share their homes with quite different animals. In New Zealand, the tuatara occasionally shares the same burrow as a shearwater. And puffins often nest in a rabbit warren. A hibernating rattlesnake may move into a marmot's burrow and remain there for the winter. To avoid its dangerous guest, if it is wise, the marmot will move to another part of the burrow.

Some animal partnerships are very successful indeed. Tick birds and cattle egrets ride on the backs of rhinoceroses and buffaloes. They feed on the tiny insects which live in the folds of thick skin. So they are useful to their large hosts. Another welcome guest is the Egyptian plover that cleans a crocodile's teeth.

Tick birds keep the rhinoceros' skin clean by eating the ticks and insects that settle in the folds.

Egrets eat the insects stirred up by the animal's hoofs.

rattlesnake and marmot

damsel fish

Egyptian plover and Nile crocodile

In a true partnership, both animal partners benefit. They may gain food, shelter, protection or a better chance of breeding successfully. Starlings may nest very close to the eyrie of a golden eagle. Their enemies are afraid of the larger bird. The eagle does not mind because the starlings give warning of intruders.

On the coral reef, the damsel fish makes its home among the stinging tentacles of a sea anemone. Other fishes would be stung to death, but the damsel fish is protected by a slimy film covering its body. But this is not a true partnership because the sea anemone does not benefit from it.

Parasites are animals that live on other animals and do them harm. In the sea, fishes like the squirrel fish, the shark and the moray eel are plagued by these pests. Fortunately, there are armies of cleaner fishes like the tiny wrasse that eat the parasites and so keep the larger fish healthy. Even the fiercest predator will open its mouth to let the cleaner fishes swim inside without harming them.

The most common partnerships are formed by a male and a female of the same animal species. When animals mate, the male and female partners may stay together all through the breeding season. They work together to build a nest or den; they feed their young and teach them to fend for themselves. Some animals, such as swans, are partners for life.

27

The pit viper is a snake that lives in the hot areas of America. They hunt at night and feed on small, warm-blooded animals. Its most important sense organs are the tiny pits on each side of its face. They sense heat from the prey's body. So the pit viper can track down a warm-blooded animal in the dark.

A fish's lateral line enables it to detect obstacles and movements in the water.

Some fishes can make electricity. They surround themselves with an electrical field. If anything moves in the field, the fishes can feel it. So they can detect their food and their enemies.

Animal Senses

Many animals have the same senses as we do. As well as sight, hearing, taste, touch and smell, they have a sense of balance and motion. And they can sense heat and cold, pain, hunger and thirst. Some animals do not have all of these senses but rely on only two or three. Others have unusual extra senses. Different creatures have developed the senses they need to stay alive.

Where an animal lives affects the kind of senses it needs. Cave-dwelling animals do not need good eyesight, but their senses of hearing and touch are

Flies have large eyes made from thousands of lenses. They are called compound eyes, and can see in all directions.

A fly's taste organs are on its feet. If it lands on sugar, it will stamp on it to check that it can be eaten before it begins its meal.

A hawk hunts for food by scanning the ground with its keen eyes. It will then hover to see what is moving before swooping down to catch a mouse.

well developed. Birds are likely to see their food from the air. They do not need to smell it, but they need good eyesight to spot it. Keen eyesight is important to many creatures. It is vital to flying insects and they have developed large compound eyes.

Most animals have the organs they need to see, hear, taste and smell in their heads. But grasshoppers have ears in their legs. And fishes sense with the lateral line along their sides.

Extra senses are sometimes used to help a fast-moving animal avoid obstacles even in complete darkness. When flying around at full speed the bat's special sense of hearing, acting rather like sonar, makes it a skillful navigator although its eyes are weak.

Moths send scent messages to each other in the dark. A male moth picks up the scent from a female with its feathery antennae.

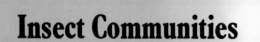

Insect Communities

Ants, bees, wasps and termites are social insects. They live together in large colonies and they are especially successful at organizing the life of their communities. In an insect society, each individual insect has a job to do. It relies on the other insects to do their jobs, too; on its own, it would soon die. An insect colony is so well-run that it behaves almost as if it were one vast "super-insect".

A few bees and wasps live alone, and they are known as "solitary" insects. But most bees and wasps build large nests. In the nest, the most important insect is the queen. The workers look after the nest and keep it clean. They take care of the eggs and feed the larvae. And they take food to the queen whose job is to lay eggs and

Although termites are not related to ants, they have a similar way of life. They are sometimes called white ants. Their huge nests are made from sand mixed with their own droppings.

control the life of the colony. In a bee hive, special workers fan their wings at the entrance to keep fresh air moving around inside.

In an ants' nest, there may be more than one queen. The worker ants have no wings but some of them have huge jaws. These are special soldier ants and their job is to defend the colony. Insect colonies may grow very large and continue to be used for many years.

Some ants burrow underground. Others build mounds of earth with a maze of tunnels inside. Ruled by a queen who spends all her time laying eggs, thousands of ants live in harmony together, working constantly to keep the colony running like an efficient machine.

Animal Language

Animals use their senses to receive messages. They use language to send messages of different kinds. A sound or a sign may attract a mate, warn of danger, show where food may be found, or indicate the limits of a territory. Whatever language is used, the message must be clear.

The language may be a sign language or one that uses body movements of some kind. Display plays an important part in the courtship of some animals. By showing off before the female, a male shows he is ready to mate. The peacock spreads his fine tail; the pigeon struts around and puffs up his neck feathers. Usually, a male bird's plumage is more colorful than the female's so he can make a fine display to attract a female at mating time.

Many animal languages use sounds. Dolphins, for instance, "talk" in high-pitched squeaks and whistles. Dogs make a lot of different noises—barks, whines, howls, snarls and so on. But a dog also uses its face and its body to communicate. While out walking, a dog will urinate at gates and lamp-posts. This is how it marks its territory. Sniffing at these scent signals, another dog can tell that other dogs are in the area. Badgers, hyenas and wolves are other animals that mark territory in this way.

In a beehive, bees communicate by making special dance movements. When a new source of pollen has been discovered, a bee will spread the good news by doing a special dance. Other bees understand exactly what the dance means. So they can find the pollen too. In an ant colony, ants communicate by tapping their antennae together.

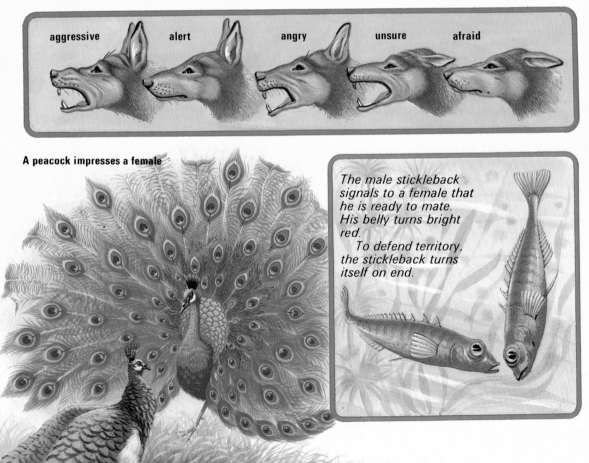

aggressive   alert   angry   unsure   afraid

A peacock impresses a female

The male stickleback signals to a female that he is ready to mate. His belly turns bright red.

To defend territory, the stickleback turns itself on end.

If a bee dances a circular dance it means that food can be found nearby.

Penguins live in the Antarctic where it is so cold that few plants can grow. So the Adélie penguins build their nests with stones. As part of its courtship display, the male penguin gives the female a pebble. If she takes it, they will build their nest together.

When two wolves meet, the "inferior" one will often cower and sniff at the other's muzzle before lying on the ground and urinating. This tells the dominant wolf that he need not fear the weak one.

Hungry wolves keep a close watch on a herd of caribou. They will attack a creature that strays from the safety of the migrating herd.

cow seal and pup

Europe

South Africa

Animal Journeys

swallow

eel

Sargasso Sea

elver

South America

In their search for food or new breeding grounds, animals often make very long journeys called migrations.

Many of the large grazing animals, such as wildebeeste, giraffe and antelope migrate to find fresh pasture. The great herds that roam the Serengeti plains in Africa follow the grass as it ripens in the rainy season. They move in a great circle, taking a year to get back to their starting point, and breeding as they travel.

Reindeer and caribou journey south in the winter to find food. They return northward in the spring. Swallows breed in North America and Europe when it is warm. They feed on flying insects. When the days shorten and there are fewer insects, the swallows fly south to South America and South Africa for the southern summer. There they remain until winter sends them north again.

There are ocean wanderers too. Seals migrate long distances across the sea to rocky islands where they mate and have their pups.

Eels make remarkable journeys. They hatch from eggs laid in the Sargasso Sea. From there, they drift across the Atlantic Ocean feeding and growing as they go. When the eels reach the coasts of Europe and America, they swim up rivers. After living in fresh water for several years, they return to the sea as adults. Then they make the long journey back to the Sargasso Sea again to mate.

Nature's Blueprints

Young animals normally look like their parents. This is because the female egg and the male sperm both have "blueprints" inside which determine what the new animal or offspring will look like. These "blueprints" are called genes.

For any one characteristic, such as the color of a flower or the color of your eyes, there will be at least two genes, one from each parent. When animals or plants reproduce, they pass on to their offspring one gene from every pair they themselves were born with.

In the diagram below, the flower labelled "pure red" has two genes for the color red. The "pure white" flower has two genes for white so it is white. A cross between these two flowers results in all the offspring having one gene for red and one for white. But because the red gene is dominant, that is, stronger, all the flowers are red.

When two such cross-bred plants reproduce, a variety of combinations

of genes may result. Here, the cross-bred plants have produced three red flowers and one white flower. One red flower has inherited two "red" genes; the other two red flowers each have one "white" and one "red" gene. They are red because the gene for red is dominant. The white flower has two "white" genes.

This example illustrates some of the basic laws of genetics as discovered by Gregor Mendel in the nineteenth century. The example opposite is more complicated.

Sometimes you see a tortoiseshell cat. Its fur is a mixture of black and ginger. The color results from the combination of a "black" gene inherited from one parent and a "ginger" gene from the other. Neither gene is dominant so both colors show. But tom (male) cats do not have two genes for these colors. They have only one. This is because all male mammals have slightly fewer genes than females. And in cats one of the male's "missing" genes is one of its "color" genes. This means that a tom will never be a tortoiseshell.

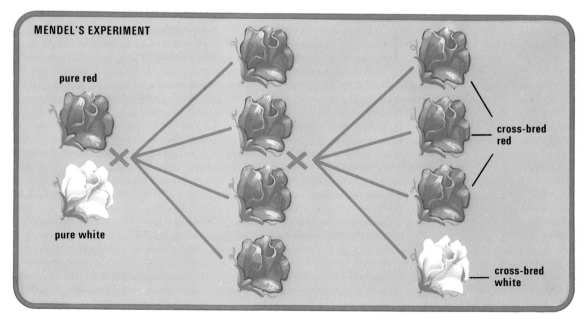

MENDEL'S EXPERIMENT

pure red

pure white

cross-bred red

cross-bred white

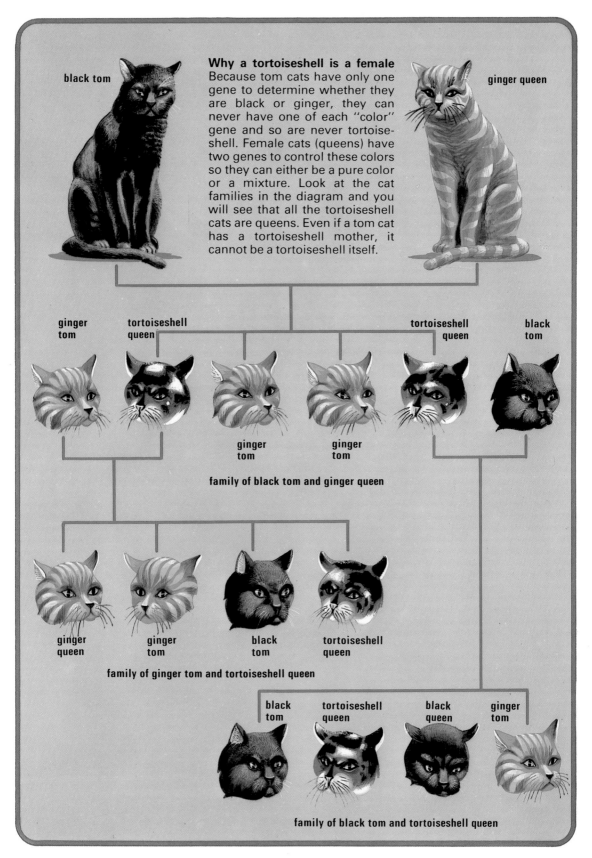

black tom

ginger queen

Why a tortoiseshell is a female
Because tom cats have only one gene to determine whether they are black or ginger, they can never have one of each "color" gene and so are never tortoise-shell. Female cats (queens) have two genes to control these colors so they can either be a pure color or a mixture. Look at the cat families in the diagram and you will see that all the tortoiseshell cats are queens. Even if a tom cat has a tortoiseshell mother, it cannot be a tortoiseshell itself.

ginger tom

tortoiseshell queen

ginger tom

ginger tom

tortoiseshell queen

black tom

family of black tom and ginger queen

ginger queen

ginger tom

black tom

tortoiseshell queen

family of ginger tom and tortoiseshell queen

black tom

tortoiseshell queen

black queen

ginger tom

family of black tom and tortoiseshell queen

Escaping the Cold

In winter, when the days are short and cold, many plants die. There is less food for animals to eat. So some migrate to warmer places where there is plenty to eat. Others escape from the food shortage and the bitter cold by going to sleep. This winter sleep is called hibernation.

It is lack of food that makes warm-blooded animals hibernate. Even though they have furry coats, they cannot keep warm without food. Cold-blooded creatures, such as reptiles and amphibians, hibernate because they would otherwise die of cold. Their bodies are always at the same temperature as their surroundings. So in freezing weather, they would freeze.

Some fishes sink to the bottom of ponds and lakes and bury themselves in the mud. Frogs, toads, newts and snakes find crevices in rocks or trees in which to escape the cold.

Before hibernating, an animal stores fat in its body. Bears, which sleep out the winter in caves, are covered with thick layers of fat in the fall. When they emerge in spring, they are much thinner and very hungry.

During its hibernation, an animal's body becomes very chilled. Its heartbeat slows down so that hardly any energy is used. The dormouse sleeps so soundly that it does not wake up even when dropped on the floor. But squirrels and hedgehogs will wake on mild winter days. Squirrels collect a store of nuts in the fall to provide food to last the winter. As soon as the weather becomes cold again, they fall asleep once more. Badgers and hedgehogs, too, may wake on milder nights. But hunters such as stoats and foxes continue prowling all winter long, often going hungry.

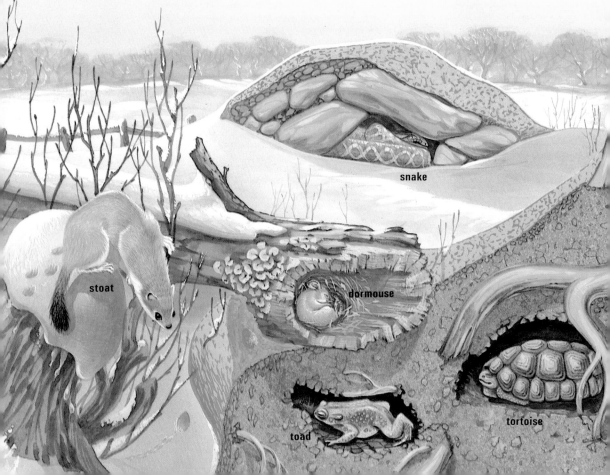

snake

stoat

dormouse

toad

tortoise

bats

Bats find a dry cave and hibernate hanging from the roof. If the temperature rises, they will fly out and feed. A bat's temperature may fall so low when it is asleep that dew forms on its fur.

squirrel

badger

brown bear

newt

hedgehog

Atkinson

Animal Adaptations

Every animal is specially equipped to suit the way it lives. Changes in the animal kingdom happen gradually by a process we call evolution. Slowly, over many millions of years, a great

live in similar conditions to true moles and mice in other parts of the world. They look very like the real thing.

When the naturalist Charles Darwin visited the Galapagos Islands in 1835, he saw a number of small finch-like birds. Some fed on seeds, others on insects. They had different beaks to

The hummingbird's long beak can probe deep into flowers for nectar.

variety of animals have evolved and changed to survive in many different environments.

Throughout nature, basic animal shapes have evolved. All insects have a three-part body: a head, a thorax and an abdomen. The thorax has three pairs of legs and sometimes wings. This "standard insect" shape has been modified to give all kinds of different insects—jumping insects like the grasshopper, swimming insects like the water boatman, flying insects like butterflies and wasps, and burrowing insects, such as burying beetles.

Animals which share a similar way of life often look alike, even though they are not related. The marsupials are confined to Australia where there are no native moles or mice. But there are marsupial "moles" and "mice" that

ptarmigan

The giraffe can reach leaves that are out of reach of other grazing animals. When they breed, the long neck pattern is passed on by chemical "messages" in the animal's cells. So all giraffes have the long necks they need to feed. Short-necked giraffes died out long ago. Today's giraffes are an example of very successful adaptation.

The peppered moth evolved into a black form for better camouflage against the bark of trees blackened by smoke.

The Arctic fox of the icy north has tiny ears which lose little heat.

The desert fox has large ears which lose heat and keep it cool.

eat these foods. But Darwin discovered that the birds were closely related. In fact, they were all descended from the "standard" finch. It had taken millions of years for the different adaptations to appear.

Fishes, birds and mammals show an amazing range of adaptations. The amphibians that first crawled out of the water on to the land developed limbs and new ways of breathing. Beaks, wings and feet on birds fit them for their different ways of living. Creatures like the ptarmigan and the stoat successfully camouflage themselves by turning white in winter. If we look carefully at animals we can see that their eyes, teeth, feet, body covering, and many other features have evolved or developed to suit the kind of life they lead.

Life in the Pond

Some of the most amazing of all nature's secrets can be discovered in a pond. Even a small sample of pond water contains a fascinating variety of life in miniature. Lots of different tiny creatures live in harmony in a pond. Their community is carefully balanced and easy to observe.

Some pond creatures can be found all the year round. Others, like the frog tadpole and the larva of the mosquito are there only at certain times of the year. The busiest time in a pond is spring or summer.

Pond animals find it difficult to breathe in the summer. When it is hot, they use up the oxygen in the water, except right at the top near the surface. The water becomes stagnant and lack of oxygen may kill some of the creatures living there. In winter, when the water freezes, many pond creatures bury themselves in the mud at the bottom of the pond. When the water warms up in spring, they come out and continue their lives.

Many insects which spend their adult lives flying about begin life in a pond or stream. The dragonfly nymph lives for a year or more under water, feeding and growing. When it is ready, it crawls up a reed stem into the sunlight and turns into an adult insect. But a host of other animals— fishes, amphibians, insects and crustaceans— spend their whole lives under water, feeding on the plants or tiny animals that abound there.

1. dragonfly
2. water beetle
3. pintail
4. frog
5. pond skater
6. caddis fly
7. frog spawn
8. water beetle
9. mosquito larvae
10. pond snail
11. common newt
12. crested newt
13. diving beetle
14. tadpoles
15. stickleback
16. diving beetle's air bubble
17. water spider
18. water boatman
19. snail eggs
20. ramshorn snail
21. caddis larvae
22. pondweed

Life on the Seashore

The plants and animals that live on the seashore have to be able to survive changing conditions. The region between high- and low-water mark is a home for a rich variety of plants and animals. The tide comes in twice a day so they are sometimes covered by salt water. For the rest of the day, they are exposed to the hot sun or the cold. They may also be soaked with rain.

Animals that live on the seashore survive when the tide is out by sheltering in rock pools or by

periwinkle

serrated wrack

spider crab

sea thong

blenny

sea lettuce

dahlia anemone

tube worm

hermit crab

common starfish

limpets

44

burrowing into the sand. Some, like limpets, whelks, winkles and barnacles, cling to rocks when the tide recedes. They feed on seaweed and find shelter fairly easily at low tide. Other hard-shelled animals, such as crabs, are well protected for life out of the water.

Animals with soft bodies, like the sea slug, fish and sea anemones, shelter in shallow pools or under rocks at low tide. They can often be found on the underside of boulders. Larger pools may harbor sea urchins or starfish. The starfish has rows of sucker feet on the underside of its arms which secure it to rocks when the tide is out.

shore crab

sea slug

mussels

bladder wrack

breadcrumb sponge

coral weed

beadlet anemone

sea urchin

prawn

barnacles

Graham Allen

Midnight World

Most animals are active during the day. But, as the sun sets, nocturnal animals emerge and take advantage of less crowded conditions. Many of these creatures have developed special night senses.

As night falls, rabbits and hedgehogs come out to feed, and foxes and badgers start their night's foraging. Bats and nightjars take to the air in pursuit of moths and other flying insects.

Unlike owls, which use their keen eyes and ears to find their prey, bats have poor eyesight. Their "sonar" helps them navigate in the darkness. Some moths can "jam" the bat's signals. They send out squeaks which confuse the bat's echo-sounding equipment long enough for the moth to escape. If a bat succeeds in catching a large moth it may carry its prey off in the fold of skin between its back legs before eating it on a perch.

The strange creatures of the deep sea live in darkness all the time. They make their own light to find mates and to lure prey within reach.

Bats use an echo sounding system to locate objects. They emit high-pitched sounds that bounce back from obstacles in their path.

Most animals of the night can see in the dark. In daylight, a cat's green eyes show slit-like pupils. But at night the pupils grow so large (to let in more light) that the eyes look black. Owls have excellent night vision. Their eyes are in the front of their heads so, unlike most birds, the owl has binocular vision—it can judge distances very accurately. Its eyes can spot any movement and its ears can detect the slightest rustle. With its broad muffled wings, the owl flies silently, giving its prey no warning before it swoops.

Owls cannot move their eyes so they have to turn and move their heads to see anything that is not directly in front of them. But the tubular shape of the owl's eye, and its large lens, mean that the owl has sharper vision than we have.

human eye

owl's eye

Secrets Quiz

1. What fish lives safely among the stinging tentacles of the sea anemone?

2. Why does a deer rub its antlers against tree trunks?

3. Some creatures carry their young on their backs. Can you name two?

4. How do honey bees help flowers to make seeds?

5. Do ladybugs eat spiders?

6. Which simple creature moves along by turning somersaults?

7. Why is it useful for a tiger to have stripes?

8. Where do eels lay their eggs?

9. How does a bee tell other bees where pollen is to be found?

10. Where are a grasshopper's "ears"?

11. What jobs does a worker bee do?

12. How does a fly taste its food?

13. Can you name six animals that hibernate?

14. What kind of animal lives in a drey?

15. What are owl pellets?

16. Why does a desert fox have bigger ears than an Arctic fox?

17. How do cats' eyes change in the dark?

18. What do we call a beaver's home?

19. What birds make their nests by sewing leaves together?

20. What do we call the process by which plants make their own food?

21. What bird is often responsible for spreading the seeds of the mistletoe plant?

22. What small mammals will eat the bark off the foot of tree trunks?

23. How does an Adélie penguin court its mate?

24. How do bats navigate?

25. A butterfly goes through two separate stages between hatching from the egg and becoming an adult. Can you name them?

26. How does the mouthbreeder protect its young from danger?

27. How does a herring-gull chick let its mother know that it is hungry?

28. Where do sea turtles lay their eggs?

29. Is a tortoiseshell cat always female?

30. What reptile can afford to lose its tail?

31. Which single-celled animal reproduces by splitting in two?

32. Does a flying squirrel really fly?

33. Why does the swift fly with its beak wide open?

34. How does a pit viper locate its prey in the dark?

35. What small bird may share a home with an eagle?

36. What are a male moth's feathery antennae used for?

The answers to these questions can be found on the following pages.
1. **27**; 2. **5**; 3. **10**; 4. **14**; 5. **17**; 6. **19**;
7. **23**; 8. **35**; 9. **32**; 10. **29**; 11. **30**; 12. **29**;
13. **38**; 14. **5**; 15. **5**; 16. **41**; 17. **47**; 18. **7**;
19. **7**; 20. **12**; 21. **15**; 22. **5**; 23. **33**; 24. **46**;
25. **8**; 26. **11**; 27. **10**; 28. **9**; 29. **37**;
30. **25**; 31. **8**; 32. **19**; 33. **21**; 34. **28**;
35. **26**; 36. **29**.